CATSPELLS

Cat Magic
through the Ages

CLAIRE NAHMAD

Illustrated by

SUSAN ROBERTSON

GRAMERCY

First published in 1998 by
Parkgate Books,
Kiln House, 210 New Kings Road, London SW6 4NZ

© Parkgate Books Ltd 1998

This edition is published by Gramercy Books,®
an imprint of Random House Value Publishing, Inc.,
201 East 50th Street, New York, New York, 10022.

Random House
New York • Toronto • London • Sydney • Auckland
http://www.randomhouse.com/

Printed and bound in China

A CIP catalogue record for this book is available from the
Library of Congress.

ISBN 0-517-16125-7

8 7 6 5 4 3 2 1

Contents

Introduction

It has been said that a cat is more a spirit than an animal. Historically, little distinction has been drawn as to the difference between witches, fairies, spirits, goddesses and the feline, for at different periods in time the cat was believed to represent them all in corporeal form.

The magical relationship between cats and witches has an ancient tradition, and in old manuscripts there is much evidence to suggest that wisewomen regarded their cat 'familiars' as founts of wisdom and occult secrets. It was believed that cats in their astral body could lead their mistresses in dreams to the source of a fund of spiritual knowledge. Indeed the physical body of a cat appears to be almost at one with its astral counterpart as it expresses the feline characteristics of celerity, silence, seeming weightlessness and the apparent ability to contemplate spectres or visions invisible to humans. In motion, the body of a cat seems to crackle with a supernatural electricity, and its ubiquity, grace and silent speed seem often to lend to it the air of a spirit rather than that of a coarse material being.

The witches and wisewomen of old believed that cats could foretell the future, predict the weather, indicate the tides of love and fortune, commune with spirits and bless magical endeavours. Whatever their individual sex, cats are inevitably associated with the spiritual feminine principle, and perhaps this is the truth which lies at the root of their soul-kinship with women and their association with witches.

The white magic worked by the wisewomen, herb-healers and charm-chanters of the past, was benign and gentle and invariably for the good of the community. Yet it is true that certain groups and individuals used the strange powers of cats for black magic and evil purposes. This division between white and black spellcraft might be responsible for the fact that in America it is generally believed that only white cats are lucky, whilst black ones serve as a portent of ill-fortune. However, it is important not to superimpose too literal an understanding of black and white magic on to the cat itself because of course it is the human agent who decides whether their powers are used for good or evil!

In Britain, black cats are considered lucky, and it is the white cat who is thought to be a creature of ill-omen. This belief seems to be related to the Celtic mother-goddess, Ceridwen, spirit of the rising moon and the stars, who, like her Scandinavian counterpart Freya, was attended by white cats who carried out her orders on earth. The Romans who invaded Britain systematically set out to destroy the power of the forest-dwelling Druidic priesthoods by spreading all sorts of fearful propaganda about them, so it seems likely that the British fear of white cats might have arisen from a terror spread abroad by these means, for the Druids revered the moon and the mother-goddess.

When we consider folklore and its many tales which feature cats, it becomes clear that cats are generally believed to bring luck, be they white, black or any other shade! There is no fear or distrust of cats in wiselore (which is thought to have come down to us from the Druidic priests and priestesses of long ago).

The Egyptians elevated cats to a regal position. To the people of ancient Egypt, cats were divine, living emblems of gods and goddesses, and to kill one, even by accident, incurred a swift and certain penalty of death upon the hapless offender. Elurus, the Egyptian cat deity, was represented by an ideograph which shows a human body surmounted by a cat's head. The cat goddess was Diana who, like the Celtic cat-goddesses, is a deity of the moon. Egyptian magic frequently called upon the cat deities, and for them the cat was ever associated with the moon, being a stalker of the night, with eyes whose pupils waxed and waned. Within Egyptian temples, cat coffins have been found dating back to the Eleventh Dynasty (2400 BC). They are of pure gold, adorned with jewels, and were crafted with consummate care and skill. Later, in the Eighteenth Dynasty, the Pharaoh built a temple in honour of cats, within which the goddess Pasht was represented by a cat's head.

Alternately venerated and tormented throughout history, cats have always retained their mystery, dignity, independence and grace. They still represent the soul of magic, secrecy and freedom. No other animal so consistently refuses all constraint. In Europe, the cat was seen as a fairy in itself, a fey creature as enchanted as any elf or spirit. Witches were supposed to assume the shape of a cat, and sometimes it was believed that cats temporarily put on the guise of a witch in order to enter the human world. When it was acknowledged that the cat and its mistress had different identities, people believed that her companion had access to magical worlds, and would escort her in her dreams to Elfame or Fairyland, from whence both would return filled with strange knowledge and mystical powers.

The spells in this book, drawn from an ancient source, are intended to cast a new light on those old beliefs and magical secrets which have always surrounded the cat. As materialism begins at last to loosen its grasp, these spells might suggest an anciently new way of observing and learning from our feline friends, and of developing a magical relationship with them, as the wisewoman did for their enlightenment and spiritual learning in a time long ago.

Naming Spells

'One for a secret, one for a riddle;
Name puss twice and befuddle the Divil . . .

(country rhyme)

The custom of bestowing several names on a person is very ancient, and has its roots in magical philosophy. The reason was that the knowledge of a name was so powerful that sorcerers, enchantresses, and even the man who hailed you on the road, might be able to gain ascendancy over you simply by familiarizing themselves with your name. The solution was to have more than one, to be kept secret from all but one's most intimate and trusted circle. This straightforward magical device was said to set the Devil a riddle, and so 'befuddle' him.

Myth and legend celebrate the concept of the mysterious power locked into names. The Egyptian goddess Isis was said to have used her magical workings to force Ra to utter his secret name, thus gaining celestial equality with the supreme sun god. The ancient Hebrew occultists studied their sacred Kabbala, in which was the Book of Numbers. Numbers were considered magical builders of the universe, and each one was assigned a letter and an astrological correlation. The special energy vibration of the sound linked to its number was considered to have a mystical power which resided in the letter and was released on utterance, rather like a genie in a bottle! The combination of letters which formed a name would, therefore, represent a potent magical tool, which could influence the narrow sphere of the personality and, when uttered by great mages who knew how to create vital thought-forms, could even affect the wider universe.

If we can accept this mystical theory, there is no reason to doubt that animals can also be influenced by their names. The old tradition of naming belongs to wisecraft, and in the following pages a list of names for cats is offered, each of which is believed to create its own 'naming-spell' if it is used in conjunction with the magical working given. The list is not comprehensive, but should serve rather as a starting point for your own ideas and research concerning the delicate question of naming your cat. Each name is supposed to impart a distinctive and individual quality, from the 'folk-names' which foster a cat's 'child-spirit' and the 'names of distinction' which lend dignity and encourage 'seniority of soul', to the 'magical name' which has guardianship over the soul of the cat. And so, according to wiselore, a subtle triune influence will be exerted over your feline friend – which celebrates naming as a magical act.

Spell for The Ancient Magical Art of Naming

When you have chosen your kitten from the kindle (litter), being sure that this little mite is the one upon whom you wish to bestow your friendship and protection, know that this is a magical pact, for you are guardian of the spirit of your cat, and he or she in like manner is invested with the occult power to guide and guard your spirit. You must think next of the naming ceremony, which is best done after some little acquaintance with the nature of your new friend.

Choose a pet-name for the cat's child-spirit, and it is better if this be a folk-name, for these names have been magically sealed with power and tradition through the ages, and the flavour of the earth is in them, and of the spirits of the earth, and of hearth and home.

Your friend may retain no more than a child-spirit all his or her life long, but let it be given a secret, occult name also, in any event, for such a name will nurture the mysteries in the cat's soul. It will protect the creature from malignant forces, will throw the Devil askew, and aid in the unfolding of his or her heart so that in the next life the animal may return with a spirit more gracious, bright and fair. And if it should be that, after a year's passing, you discover unto yourself that your cat has indeed already achieved seniority of soul, then it is meet that the animal should be given a grander name, to inspire, foster and encourage the qualities that are beginning to reveal themselves, so that this treasure-hoard may grow and grow, and come to shine with a divine brilliance like the stars of the night.

Do not hesitate to give your cat three names, for there is the inspiration of the Holy Trinity in it, and cats especially are animals of the Soul of All Things. To name a cat three times whispers too of

the triform nature of the moon, for does not the
night-goddess appear to us with either a full round
face, or waxing with horns towards the east, or yet
waning with horns towards the west? And in her
pretty crescent or her majestic fullness, do we not
see a likeness when we study the cat's eye, for does
not the contraction and dilation of its pupil speak
to us of Bride and Artemis, goddesses of the new
moon and the full? The cat is ever the creature of
the night and the goddess of the night.

To name puss, it is well to choose one of the
Egyptian days of our calendar, and to gather
valerian to make into a few drops of oil, so that you
may anoint him or her just on the tip of the nose
and behind the ears.

An old manuscript says 'Three days there are in the year which we call Egyptian days', and this is so because they were days of great divinity and consequence to the astrologers of ancient Egypt. These three days fall on the last Monday in April, the second Monday in August and the third Monday in December.

All of the Egyptian days are Mondays, that is, days of the moon; and so we may call upon Butis, the goddess of night, Diana, the goddess of the ascended moon, Isis, the goddess of the moon at her rising, and Sekhmet, the Lady of Flame, for she is of vital power, a seer by night, and a goddess of might whose inspiration fires the mind and elevates it to acts of hermetic magic and woman's wisecraft.

On such an Egyptian night, take puss in your arms and stand in some sequestered place, wild and lovely, where you may see the moon as she rides the skies. Have a little phial of valerian oil ready in the pocket of your apron, and scatter a few drops around yourself upon the turf to make a magic circle. Call upon the four angels Kokaviel, Ghedoriah, Chokmahiel and Savaniah, for these angels are of Mercury's messenger spirit, and he is Lord of Naming. Call down the blessing of the goddesses of the night, and imagine yourself to be standing in a pure white temple, framed by magic's skill.

Anoint puss, and tell the baptismal name to the stars, afterwards proclaiming thus:

'Your name I set upon your brow
And to four shining angels bow
This mark of grace your guardian be
And make your name a magic key
Goddesses of Moon and Might
Bless my spells this Egypt's night.'

The spell is now worked. After thanking the angels, spirits and goddesses who worked with you, and bowing three times to the moon and the stars, you may 'homewards wend your way', deservedly satisfied with the night's enterprise and your weaving of woman's mysteries.

Names to Impart Distinction

'To honour the dignity of your feline companion, and to bestow consequence'

Feminine

ADELINE
'Noble serpent': for a queen who is shy, sensitive, easily offended, quiet and unobtrusive.

AGATHA
'Goodly': for a queen who is primarily reserved and proud, over whose spirit move vivid flashes of brilliance; who in rare and intimate moments is lively and kittenish.

ALBERTA
'Nobly bright': for a queen who is retiring, independent, graceful; who has a pensive, dreamy air as though she lived half in the spirit world; who distrusts men.

ANGELICA
'Angelic': for a queen who loves the moon and whose behaviour accurately foretells the weather; who must be stirring at night, who seems to see fairies; during the day she is languid and voluptuous; her affections run deep.

AURELIA
'Golden': for a queen who is haughty, flighty in her affections, beautiful in appearance, adores home-comforts and luxury; she is disdainful of other cats.

AWNE
'Swan-maiden' (Awne or Aine was the fairy goddess of the Celts): for a

queen with a sparkling, humorous air, as though she were ever laughing joyously at her human friend; her affections are sentimental, she has grace and beauty, she is an ever-faithful companion to one member of the family, whom she herself selects.

BEATRICE

'Blesser': for a queen who is lively, bold, intelligent and gay; she is enterprising and determined, she often finds herself in trouble, but is cheerful and imaginative in her attempts to extricate herself from it.

BERENICE

'Bringer of victory': for a queen who is full of vanity and selfishness, yet is the soul of constancy and who unconsciously brings much laughter and amusement to her human friend.

BRIDGET

'Virgin bride, strength': for a queen who is peaceful, homely, domesticated and devoted; she cherishes motherhood and is fiercely protective of her young; her owner has her heart above all else, however, from whom she will accept even abuse quietly and meekly.

CLEMENTINA

'Merciful': for a queen who is a good mother, affectionate, loyal and placid; she is sleepy, but not indolent; she will catch prey, but only for food; she is attracted to water.

COLUMBINE

'Dove': for a queen who is timid, resourceful, hesitant and solitary; her trust can be enticed from her, and if you are worthy, it is yours for good.

DIANA

'Goddess': this queen is a strong, proud, vital animal; her passions and affections are deeply rooted, and will never fail; she is never fickle, but always valorous and bold; she may seem to have magical powers and to be in communion with spirits; it is easy, and instructive, to converse with the soul of this cat.

ELFRIDA

'Elf-threatener': solitary, proud, dignified, this queen prefers her own company; the human friend is sometimes graciously allowed to engage her affectionate attention; she is elegant, delicate, graceful, reserved; she needs to know you well before she will place her trust in you.

ERNESTINA

'Eagle stone': for a queen who is animated, coquettish, ardent in her affections; her air is one of vulnerability, surprise and timidity; she can show great courage, however, in the face of danger, and suffers pain or injury with reticence and forbearance.

GRISELDA

'Stone battle maid': this queen is resourceful and determined; she possesses an abundant, muscular beauty; she is fearless and graceful; her soul is remote and strong; but she is deeply faithful.

PETRONELLA

'Rock': for a queen who is jealous in her affections, arrogant, restless and alert; she is intelligent, passionate and regal; she is a conscientious though excitable mother.

ROSAMUND

'Rose of the world': for a queen who is spiritual, refined and delicate in her habits; pensive, dreamy, beautiful and proud of carriage; in her affections she is gentle, yielding and ardent.

SELENE

'Moon': for a queen who is secretive, drawn to the night, dark and mysterious in her aspect, majestic, gracious, condescending; she is serene and inert during the day; her habits are luxurious and extravagant.

SIBYL

'Wisewoman': for a queen who seems to be possessed of an ancient, steadfast soul; sagacious, calm, refined, sweet-natured; she prefers

quiet seclusion in the company of
her owner, to whom she is
passionately devoted, although she
has a strong, independent,
resourceful personality.

THEODORA

'Divine gift': for a queen who is
sweet of temperament, graceful,
wistful; she is intuitive emotional
and timid; her human friend will
often dream of her; her dream-
likeness is wise and full of strange
prophetic powers.

VIRGINIA

'Maidenly': for a queen who is
serious, attentive, silent and
graceful; she is unassuming, but can
be tempestuous when aroused; she is
generally timorous and of subtle,
changing moods.

ZERAH

'Rising of light': for a queen who is
whimsical, seeming to dwell in a
world of visions, she is intelligent,
proud and austere; her personality is
daring, captivating; she can be
impetuous and intrepid.

Masculine

ALFRED

'Wise elf in council': for a tom who
is prudent, keen, cunning and wise;
he is strong and bold, solitary and
pensive; he does not make enemies
but is held in deep respect; even dogs
flee him.

AMBROSE

'Immortal': for a tom who is
affectionate, trustful, languid,
voluptuous and extravagant in
personality; he loves the night, seeks
a mate, but avoids fights; he is a
first-rate hunter, but will kill only
for food; he is deeply crestfallen
and subdued if he loses his
dignity.

AUBREY

'Elf ruler': for a tom who seeks the
company of the moon and the night;
he may be away for days, yet
always returns faithfully home,
with a sagacious air, as though his
travels have imparted much
experience and wisdom; if he has a
feline companion, he will become
deeply attached to his friend; his
owner can be sure of his affection
and loyalty.

BERTRAND

'Bright raven': for a tom who is wise
and noble in his bearing, whose eyes
hold great depth, who seems to hold
counsel with himself as though he

could gaze steadily down the highways of time and garner wisdom from ages past; he will walk with you, and guide you to strange and lovely places where the fairies dwell; he is always gentle and affectionate and devoted to his owner, although he can be fearless when the need arises.

CARADOC

'Beloved': for a tom who is bright, humorous and agile; he displays a sweet kittenish temperament, although his human friend is not fooled, for this cat is wise and gifted; he can enter your dream as a guiding beneficent spirit; he is not afraid of losing his dignity, and seems often to seek to do so, as though he had some lesson to impart to his delighted observers.

CARMICHAEL

'Friend of Michael': for a tom who is erratic, noble, ubiquitous; he is agile and intelligent, his temperament is like quicksilver; full of surprises and quirks; he is affectionate, though reserved.

DOMINIC

'Sunday's child': for a tom who is loveable, changeable, though unswerving in his loyalty to his owner; he distrusts men and adores women, almost as if he would pay court to them; he chooses certain stations in his environment which become his indisputable domain; for this principle to be challenged causes him the deepest consternation, and such effrontery will cause him to leave home for a period as a chastisement to his owner. Yet being loyal, he will always return, expecting to be petted and made much of.

EGBERT

'Formidably bright': for a tom who is sensitive, intelligent, proud of his status among his fellows; he has no sense of humour, and mishaps and misjudgements cause him agonizing humiliation and embarrassment; if his owner is party to his fall from dignity, he will sulk for hours. Being a noble tom; he is delicate and honourable in his habits and behaviour.

JABEZ

'Sorrow': for a tom who is gentle, affectionate, loyal and placid; his is a solitary soul, but he will never stray far from home, as though he were cognizant of life's shadows; he is contemplative, meek and unobtrusive; nice in his habits.

JEROME

'Holy name': for a tom who is impulsive, rash, haughty; he loves to dice with death, especially when he has an audience; he loves the night and the moon, but is very companionable at home; his enemies fear him; he loves human companions of the feminine gender and generally will not allow caresses from men; he is honourable in battle, and will allow vanquished foes to escape without harm; he is very jealous and possessive with his human family.

LLEWELLYN

'Lionlike': for a tom who is sleek, muscular, noble and upright of carriage; he is never furtive; he loves company, but is reserved and watchful therein; strangers make him shy; rare moments find him adoringly affectionate towards his human friend; he has ever a warm heart beating beneath a cool and poised exterior.

MARMADUKE

'Sea leader': for a tom who is a traveller, an adventurer, who seems to wish to walk the wide world; he seeks many lady-loves, for whom he would fight to the death; after many wanderings, he will come home to enjoy the peace and company of the domestic fire, fully expecting to be cosseted, fussed over, petted and fondled as if he were a warrior home from the battlefield. His owners generally meet his expectations, for they sense a spirit of expansiveness and nobility in him.

OTTO

'Rich': for a tom who is fond of capers and games; he is athletic, enthusiastic, innocent, valorous and cheerful; he will seldom allow his owner to be idle, demanding constant attention and active companionship; he likes to shadow his human friend, yet will, by and by, settle and grow placid and indolent for a little while; he dreams vividly, and can step into the dreams of his human companion.

RANDOLPH

'Wolf of the house': for a tom who is exuberantly loyal, affectionate, sweet-natured and sociable; he is noble, wise, strong, intelligent and physically majestic; has moments of gravity and contemplation, but is more often absurdly kittenish, loveable and playful.

SOLOMON

'Peaceful': for a tom who is languorous, luxurious, proud, extravagant and delicate in his habits; he presents an air of aristocratic refinement, as though he were cultured and high-bred; he adores his human family, who alone can induce him to relax his dignity and become playful.

THEODORIC

'Ruler': for a tom who is passionate in his freedom and independence, who is individualistic, eccentric, phlegmatic and wise; he has periods of domesticity, when he is abundantly and overtly affectionate.

Folk-Names for Feline Child-Spirits

BILLY WINKER
(Lancashire spirit – child guardian)
Perifool, Terrytop, Tom-Tit-Tot
(benign Celtic fairy spirits): for a
tom who is winsome, mischievous,
easily frightened, often foolish; he
stalks prey assiduously, but will
turn around and run when he gets
too close to his quarry.

KITTY-WITCH
(Celtic fairy): for the queen who is
pert, capricious, frolicsome, moody;
she plays the coquette to gain
human attention, frisks at weather
changes and thunder, becomes
irritable and demanding if she
cannot remain the centre of
attention.

MELSH DICK
(Guardian spirit [male] of nut
copses): for a tom who is swift and
silent as a sprite, always appearing
unexpectedly or spying on his
human friends from hidden peep-

holes; he is disobedient, cheerful and
heedless; he causes many minor
calamities; he loves the night, and he
loves to be vocal in it.

PEGSY
(Guardian spirit [female] of nut
copses), Jinty (nursery fairy),
Kara Dia (lunar spirit), Gillsie
(nursery spirit): for a queen who is
timid, frisky and shy; she dislikes
company and will flee at the sight of
strangers; her owner will be able to
win her trust only with great effort
and patience; she needs to be steadied
and brought down to earth.

PISKY
(Celtic fairy), Asrai (water fairy):
for a queen who is of shifting
moods; she will assume a regal air,
then wax kittenishly playful; she
will sulk for an hour or two, fall
asleep, and wake wide-eyed
and innocent, forgetful of
presumed insults.

WIGGIN

(Celtic fairy): for a tom who is playful, foolish and unable to acquire the usual feline skills; he cannot climb, unless it be to the window-ledge, where he spends most of his time; he is prone to absurd mishaps and accidents which are seldom serious; he cannot hunt, but will run after butterflies.

WILKIE

(Celtic fairy), Skillywidden, Tom Cockle, Whuppity Stoorie: for a tom who is phlegmatic, plodding, patient; he will insist on attempting what he knows he is incapable of, and has often to be rescued from treetops and other heights; he will always flee from a fight, though other toms seek to waylay him.

YARTHKINS

(Fertility spirit): for a queen who is playful, affectionate and kittenish all her life, although she kindles many kittens; these she hides with great mystery in odd places, presenting them afterwards to her human friend with a show of triumph and pride in her achievement.

Magical Names
Queens

ARIANRHAD
Goddess of human destiny, and spiritual guide; she is the mother of weaving and webs, also known by the Celtic name Isis.

ASTARTE
'Goddess of the moon with crescent horns.'

AURORA
Goddess of the dawn and of rising stars.

BRIDE OR BRIDGET
The new moon.

CYNTHIA
The waxing moon.

DIANA
The moon which rides the open vault of the firmament (waxing, as 'Cynthia'), 'hunting the clouds'.

EASTRE
The waning moon, almost full, when she shows the form of a hare upon her eroding disc.

FREYA
The full moon with a maiden's face.

HEBE
Goddess of youth who wielded the power of eternal beauty and renewal; she restored youth to the aged, and was celestial cup-bearer to the gods.

HECATE
The waning moon.

ISHTAR
The fertility goddess of Babylon whose sigil (symbol) is Venus, the lovely and tranquil evening star.

ISIS
Mother of Horus, the rising sun; she is a moon goddess, and her magic is the act of becoming, of initial appearance; her sacred arts are spinning and weaving.

LUNA
The full moon, goddess of the night, who loved the sleeping shepherd Endymion, symbol for humanity.

MORRIGAN
The dark side of the moon.

PHOEBE
The moon as pale sister of the sun.

RUTHVAH
The spiritual essence of immortality and the Supernal Triad.

SESHETA
Egyptian goddess of writing, philosophy and inspiration; she was the great founder of temples and holy places.

Toms

ABRA MELIN
Great occultist who was author of an ancient collection of magical writings ('The Sacred Magic of Abra Melin the Mage').

ABRAXAS
One of the mythical horses who draw the Dawn-Chariot, he is the spirit of each passing year.

AGRIPPA
A mage from Britain's ancient past who worked with angels and spirits; he created a sacred seal of healing.

AMEN RA
Supreme Egyptian god – patron of Pharaohs, lord of truth, omnipotent god of Thebes; his name is the Sacred Word recognized by all mystics and spellcrafters.

CERNUNNOS
God of ancient forests, whose spirit dances in the shaded grottoes and

serene twilight glades of deepest evening.

ELIPHAS LEVI
Master occultist, 'the last of the Magi', who imparted the Star of the Magi to the occult world (one of the great mysteries).

ETHON
One of the sacred horses of the sun.

GABRIEL
Angel of the moon and lord of the lunar spirits.

HORUS
The hawk-headed Egyptian day-god, spirit of the rising sun and lord of its path from dawn to eve.

MERLIN
Celtic wizard, 'Prince of Enchanters'.

OSIRIS
Husband to Isis and Egyptian god of the moon, waning stars, sinking sun and setting planets; he is, according to Egyptian lore, lord of the kingdom of ghosts and judge of the dead.

PYTHAGORAS
One of the great magicians; an angel came to him to impart the secrets of life.

THOTH
Egyptian god of magic and enchantments.

Healing Spells

'Brother, put away your groans;
I bring a black-cat charm to mend your bones.'

(proverb)

The cat has always been associated with magic spells for healing, and although its use in charms, spellcraft and simples (as for instance when cat hairs are an ingredient of a magical herbal posy) often amounts to little more than ensuring its presence whilst the sorcery is put into operation, there is a quiet insistence throughout folklore that special enchantments require the inspiration of a cat, perhaps because they seem to know the world of spirits so well.

There are in existence many charms and spells which call for cruel treatment of the cat. My own feeling is that these are aberrations, products of black magic that have sometimes muddied the waters of authentic wiselore, which has its genesis in the teachings of the Druids. The Druidic priests and priestesses are believed by many people nowadays to have been vegetarian, and to have abhorred the ill-treatment of animals. Pythagoras, who himself was much drawn to the healing arts, is believed to have drawn great inspiration from the Druids, and to have expounded the doctrine of vegetarianism and the humane treatment of animals.

For the purposes of these spells, the cat's presence, a few hairs from its coat, or the anointing of it by water or oil are all that is required. The cat's tail figures prominently, as it was believed that this part of the creature's anatomy was a kind of charm-wand, a quivering antenna into the spirit worlds, through which the cat received intelligence and visitation from such realms.

In the text, the cat as magical assistant is referred to throughout as 'she', but of course this female chauvinism does not exclude toms from such ceremonies!

The angelic charms and spells might be of particular interest as we stand upon the threshold of the new age. If we are to grow in spiritual stature, imagination is truly the key, because until we begin to use it there is a blockage in our psychic vision. Animals, especially cats, who are almost astral creatures, facilitate human contact with spirits. This can be achieved by making a conscious, relaxed effort to reach into a higher state of awareness, by responding positively to beauty in nature, music and art, and by calling upon the clarity and simplicity of the feline soul.

The angelic charms offer a starting-point for such communion – a chance to grasp the handle and begin to turn it . . .

Charm to Mend Broken Bones

To encourage broken bones to heal quickly, and to
take away the pain, recite this charm over them
after they have been set, whilst stroking a black cat:

'Blessings on your skull;
With holy secrets it is full;
Let it smile on these bones
Precious as earth's stones
Let it bless these bones
And hush your groans;
Let it work the spell
To knit these bones and make them well.
Blessings on your skull
With holy secrets it is full.'

Gather a little hair from the cat (let it be loose hair,
do not hurt her) and put it in a little white linen
bag, which is to be worn around the neck until the
bones are well on the mend. Bless the cat with her
magical name.

The Veil of Isis Cat Spell

If anyone in the home should fall sick, take a crystal bowl filled with well-water and wash the hands and the face of the patient in it. Then carry it to the garden door, and call for the cat of the household. When she appears, say to her:

'Cat spirit, bright as sixpence,
Chase the devil a long long distance;
His soul I hold in these drops of water –
May he be routed before next moon's quarter.'

Then you must throw the water away onto the garden, so that it passes over puss but does not fall on her. She will, as likely as not, run away as if in pursuit of some spirit, and for this you must thank her three times over by using her magical name. In throwing the water over her to the ground, you have created the magical veil of Isis, which summons the demon of the illness and draws it away from your loved one so that the cat may carry it away from the house. Before the next moon's quarter, that is, before a week has passed away, the one who has fallen sick should be on the mend.

Charm to Cure a Wart

If you should have warts, be patient and wait till a morning in the month of May, if you would cure yourself by the agency of a cat; but it must be a tortoiseshell cat, and you must be good friends with her. Stroke the wart three times with the tip of her tail, which she will allow if you nurse her as you do it. Then chant:

'May Moon, May Moon,
May this wart wane to your tune.'

Then, as the May moon wanes, your wart will disappear.

Angelic Charm to Ward Off Listlessness and Fatigue, and to Drive Away the Blue Devils

To work this mystical charm, you must go out by night into the wilds, upon a Tuesday, the day of Mars, which happens to fall upon a night of the waxing moon. Carry puss with you to bless your endeavours, for you will summon the spirits through her.

Take six white candles with you, and when you come to a fair place, where you can see Diana's moon hunting the high clouds, mark out a magic circle with the candles, taking care to build a supporting ring of stones around each one so that nothing can catch fire, and light them from right to left.

With puss in your arms, you must pace sunwise (clockwise), intoning to the angels:

'Bartzachiah, nobly bright,
Grant me health and courage tonight.
Angelic spirit Eschiel
In your heart all courage dwells.
Angel Ithuriel
May all harms thy spirit quell.

Lovely Angel Madimiel
May good cheer come to bless me well.
Madimiel, Ithuriel, Eschiel and Bartzachiah
I thank you, spirits of Divine Fire.'

Blow out your candles, and bow to the moon, for you must never forget the goddess of the night. Before the next new moon, your weariness will be banished, your confidence restored, and your spirits refreshed.

Angelic Charm for Sleeping

If at night you take puss to sleep at the foot of your bed, and enclose a little posy of rosemary, lavender and valerian in a charm-bag which you will leave open upon your pillow, and call upon your friend to lead you into dreamland, taking care to use her magical name; and if you pray to the angel Iachadiel, and drink deep of the fragrance of the posy, then your sleep will be enchanted, your questions answered, and the souls of your departed will be summoned unto you. It is best if this spell be essayed upon a Wednesday, day of wisdom.

Qualway Cat Spell

Here is a little charm to summon a spirit to take away a stye in the eye. Capture puss and sit her on your knee. When she is comfortable, gently take the tip of her tail into your left hand, and stroke your eye softly with it, intoning:

> *'I poke thee, now I don't poke thee,*
> *I charm the queff that's under the 'ee;*
> *O qualway, O qualway!'*

A gentleman must use a queen, and a tom must be for a lady, and in both instances the cat must be black.

Angelic Charm to Break All Enchantments and to Protect From Injury

To work this charm, you need only sit with your cat in your bedchamber under Bride's new moon, watching the stars. Have a little phial of rose-water at your elbow, made holy by a blessing. Speak thus to the great angel Sophiel:

'Shining Angel Sophiel
Work for me this goodly spell;
All glamour and evil enchantments break
And guard me when I sleep and wake;
Bless my friendship with this cat,
May our hearts ne'er closeness lack.'

Take the phial of rose-water and anoint your animal friend with three drops. The cat is likely to clean herself, which is a fortunate sign. Listen in your heart to the wisdom your friend will impart to you, for you shall share many secrets, and she shall reveal unto you many things which you could learn from no other source.

Charm for the Toothache

Find the cat of the house whilst she is washing, and sprinkle salt around her three times sunwise and three times widdershins (that is, clockwise and anti-clockwise) and beseech her thus:

'Little one, fly to your Lady;
Have her work this charm for me;
There is a fire within my tooth,
Her gentle magic can surely soothe.'

Thank your cat using her magical name, and her spirit will fly to Diana, the cat-goddess, who will take away your pain as the moon rises. You must bow to the moon three times that night and intone with all solemnity:

'Diana, Lady of the Moon
Enchantments you weave on your silver loom;
I thank you for your spell today
Which took my aches and pains away.'

Charm for a Scald

If you should scald yourself, fill a bowl with water and make the sign of the cross over it, then call to the household cat. When she comes, you must gently pull a few loose hairs from her coat, and place them in the water. As they float, you must blow them away from the centre where you made the sign of the cross, and say to the angels:

'There came three angels from out of the East;
One brought fire and two brought frost;
Out fire, in frost,
In the Name of the Father, Son and Holy Ghost.'

Throw the water away over the cat (so that it does not touch her) and end the spell by intoning:

'Great Mother of All, who brings the rain,
Put out my fire, put out my pain.'

Thank the Godhead, and bless your cat in its magical name. So shall the spell be worked.

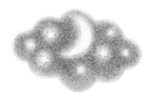

Spells for Love and Enchantments

'Whenever the cat of the house is black,
The lasses of lovers will have no lack.'

(country proverb)

The cat's occult associations have inspired such strong fascination that it has come to be a symbolic expression of female mystery and sexuality. Love divination and love spells anciently required the magical presence of a cat, who was once believed to be so familiar with the secrets of the heart that people would try to avoid conversing within earshot of one, in case it overheard their confidence and cast some spell over their fate and fortune.

The significance of cats in the sorcerous arts is undeniable, and we find their close involvement in spells of the deepest, most evocative kind, as well as in simple country spells, which also include many other kinds of animals. Cats are unique in that the people of one of the most magical societies ever to have existed, the ancient Egyptians, venerated them and included them in their most secret, esoteric rituals. Indeed, Diana, queen of the moon and cat-goddess, was an Egyptian deity. When a household cat died, its owner would perform funeral rites for it and shave off his eyebrows as a token of mourning. Cat souls were considered to be on a par with human souls, and their role in the mysteries was equal in significance and standing to that of human beings. In many ways, the ancient Egyptians considered them to be a superior race to their own.

The 'spells for enchantments', which involve calling upon the angelic hierarchy, working magic to summon spirits, and the creation of effigies, are different in kind to the spells perpetuated by exoteric folklore. They are deeper, more mysteriously occult, and have an air of witchcraft and the essence of high magic which is worked from scholarly grimoires.

Because of this, it seems fitting that there is now an astrological cat. Although the starry figure is little known, the zodiacal cat certainly does exist in the form of Faelis, the Heavenly Feline. It was depicted by the astronomer Lalande at the beginning of the nineteenth century, and was formed from a group of stars which stretched between Antlia (the Air Pump) and Hydra (the Water Snake). The cat is depicted as if in repose, with its tail wrapped around the right side of its body, and its two front paws slightly apart. Joke or not, it does somehow seem fitting that the black cat, luck-bringer, familiar of witches and companion of spirits, has at last attained celestial status!

A Spell to Gain Entry Into the Worlds of Artistic Inspiration, Visions and Dreams

Choose a Wednesday, which is Mercury's day, and choose the magical hour of six o'clock. Anoint a pale blue and a pale silver candle with rose-oil, and scatter rose petals, dried or fresh, upon your altar.

Light the candles and as you kindle them, call your cat to you, so she sits nearby.

Take some hairs from her coat and burn them in the candle flame so that a sharp incense mingles with the fragrance of the rose-oil. This is the perfume of the cat-goddess, Pasht or Diana, who presides in rites where a cat is present. Say to the goddess:

'Diana, shelter me in your wings
Inscribe around me three magic rings.'

Then you may begin the rite proper. As you inhale the sweet incense from the yellow-flamed candles, imagine a world of radiance opening up in the heavens, as though you studied the open heart of a jewel. You will see four shining angels therein. Address them thus:

'Spirits Chasan and Phorlakh
Draw my soul like the rising lark;
Arel and Talishad
Be thou my spirit's guard.'

As the angels offer you their blessings, so you will feel the fetters and the earthly bonds fall away. You will enter worlds sublime, dangerous and beautiful; worlds filled with an exquisite poignance which will break your heart so you may discover unearthly treasure beneath its exterior – a new heart which looks with inward eyes on to vistas divine. Watch until your candles burn away; and as their flame rises into smoke, know that your own soul's essence is aspiring ever upwards.

After you have rested, begin your artistic work, first bowing to the moon and thanking the angelic spirits for their cooperation and heavenly love. So shall you work and accomplish much that you thought impossible.

Let your cat remain by your side as you work; for she holds a subtle link which must not be broken.

Cat Spell to See Spirits

Find three black candles, and set up an altar by moonlight, and call puss into your room so that you may enlist magical protection from her.

Begin to melt the wax slowly in a crystal bowl, taking care that it should not overheat. When it is malleable, shape it into the image of a black cat and set it upon the table. Pluck three hairs from your head and set them about the neck of the cat like a collar. Anoint the effigy with rose-oil, and mark the sign of the cross upon its head. Finally, take some hairs from your cat, and press them into the soft wax.

You must fill this image with your magical intention to understand and love the soul and the spirit of your cat, for that is what the effigy represents. By this occult act of bonding, your cat friend is now your familiar, for you have declared your intent to the spirits.

For aid in divination and communion with spirits, you must call upon the angel Parasiel, who is Lord and Master of Treasures:

'Lord Parasiel, throw open wide the doors of my soul;
May all my visions be chaste and whole.'

After this invocation, you will feel a sense of purity flowing into your deepest heart, and you will begin to draw close to the spirits. Light a white candle dressed with oil of rosemary, and you will begin to see them one by one as they appear to you in the room. The sight will be strange and mysterious indeed, and hauntingly lovely; but do not allow yourself to become afraid.

Speak to the spirits, and they will converse with you. Your messages will be exchanged within your heart. When the midnight hour has passed, snuff out your candles and bring the magical working to a close, taking care to thank the spirits for their presence.

Spell to Call up a Hearth-Spirit

For your dwelling-place to be a true home, a household spirit needs to live within its walls. So that a good brownie may be induced to take up residence, take puss on one side, and utter this magic charm over her head three times:

'Little one, without a name
Come inside and make much game;
I send my cat upon this errand
To hunt you out till you be found
And may you of good heart be
And truly charming company.'

Then let puss run off, and when she comes home again you must watch her closely; you will see her skit and play, patting a little at the air, and growing kittenish as though a child played with her.

So by little signs and signals you will come to recognize that a brownie has entered your house; and you may be confident that he will soon make himself known to you. Never frighten or abuse him, but thank him for the tasks he performs, and always praise his handiwork.

The Mirror, The Cat and The Moon Lovespell

Here is a spell to be essayed on Walpurgis Night, which is fair Mayday's Eve. Coax your cat to go with you to a pond or a rushing stream, and take with you a mirror, a man's silk handkerchief and a white candle with some tinder to light it.

When you reach the water's edge, light the candle hold it up to the moon, and intone this rune:

'Lovely Freya, Queen of the Moon
Bring my true love to me by the month of June.'

As the moon rises, call puss and let her study her wide-eyed face in the mirror for a little while. Then turn your back to the water and hold the mirror aloft so that it reflects the moon, and also her reflection on the water. Place the silk handkerchief

over your face and count the number of moons
which appear in the mirror. If there are but two, a
twelvemonth must pass by before you are wed, but
if there are more, their number represents the
months which must pass away before you are wed.

If your cat is strong in magic, your true love's face
will appear in the mirror, as still as the reflection of
the moon, just for an instant.

The Loveletter Cat Spell

Whenever you go to post a letter to your love, call to your cat to accompany you on your walk. Then your letter will be sure to reach its destination, and will impart your message of love as you meant your beloved to understand it.

Spells for Good Luck

'May sweet delight be this month's theme —
I saw a cat in last night's dream . . .'

(country rhyme)

Cats are traditional luck-bringers, although their goodwill must be fostered and respected. The reason why they are so revered as omens of good fortune has been lost in the mists of pre-history. However, fantastic claims have been made for cats' origins, not least that they came to earth long ago from another planet and another dimension.

In some places, fear of cats persists, however, and the idea of them having their genesis in the dark bowels of the earth, might linger to influence miners and seamen, for both are superstitious about pronouncing the word 'cat' when underground or at sea. Sailors favour them as luck-bringers, even so, and to throw one overboard is said to raise a witch-storm at sea. Actors believe that to kick a cat, or to abuse it verbally, brings bad luck to their performance. They are happy to have an established theatre-cat, and for it to run about behind stage, but if it actually crosses the stage, dire misfortune will be visited on the theatrical production.

It was once thought unlucky to 'flit a cat', or to remove it with the rest of the family when they moved house. Such a superstition seems to be connected with the idea of avoiding the anger of domestic spirits and hearth brownies, who often became attached to the household cat, sometimes using their body as a vehicle. This tradition still seems to be honoured today in some cases, although the custom would certainly seem to be an abusive one.

Although the magical powers of the cat can be used for good or ill according to human purposes, people once held the belief that cats could be intrinsically evil. Attitudes seemed to sway between desiring them as household companions because of their luck-bringing properties and visiting cruelty on them because they were associated with the Devil. They were thought to harbour evil spirits, and if a cat fell ill, however harmless the disease to human beings, they were put outside in the belief that the demons of their sickness would pursue the entire family. These unkind customs have almost died out, prevailing only in a few rural communities today.

The cat, however, with its nine lives, is a resilient creature. These good-luck spells honour its dignity and its appeal, and obviate those superstitious practices which arose from penalizing the unfortunate cat for human failings.

The Cait Sith Good Luck Charm

For good luck and protection, it is well to call upon the Highland Fairy Cat, the Cait Sith.

Bind around your forehead, inside your bonnet, a bouquet of the mystic herbs chicory, henbane and rue, and go by night to the summit of a small hill, or a grassy knoll. Place seven white stones in a circle around you, and bless each one. Stand in the centre and perform a song for the fairies. Say aloud before you begin: 'This is for the fairies.'

When you have finished, bow three times to the moon, and say aloud:

'Fairies, I have danced for you,
Fairies, I have sung for you;
Now, I pri'thee, send to me
The Fairy Cat, the spirit Cait Sith (pronounced 'shee')
My guide and safeguard for to be.'

Having chanted the charm three times, you must cast the henbane upon the hill where you have danced; and you must take home with you the seventh stone from which you formed your magical circle, and the chicory and rue which comprised two parts of the nosegay bound about your brow.

When you are home, brew yourself a tisane (tea)

from the herbs, and go at once to your bedchamber
to drink it, carrying the seventh stone with you.

Bless the stone with the sign of the holy cross,
anoint it with three drops of water from the tisane,
and finish the rest before slipping into bed.

Once there, drop the stone beneath your bed at
its head, so that its place on the floor corresponds
with your pillow. Say the charm again three times
before sleeping, and as you begin to dream, the Cait
Sith will come to you and make itself known to you.

Never take the stone away from beneath your
bed, letting it remain directly below the point
where your head lies; and if it should happen that a
little stray cat presents itself to you, take it in, for it
will harbour the spirit of the Cait Sith, and you
may call upon the Cait Sith, and know that you
have a friend and protecting spirit at all times.
Thank the fairies for this, and the kindly goddess of
the moon, who is mother to all mortals.

The Black Cat Welcoming Charm

If a black cat should come of its own accord into your home, either through a window or an open door, that is very lucky and a good omen indeed. It is right to welcome the cat, and to try to persuade it to remain as the household pet. To welcome it as is meet, chant this rune three times over the cat as you stroke it:

'Black cat, black cat
Luck-bringer and blessing
Where it is that thou art from
Can only keep us guessing
Your soul we claim upon this day
We bid you never, never stray
Abide with us and here to stay
We chant this charm, you must obey
Black cat, black cat,
Luck-bringer and blessing.'

When this is done, pluck some valerian and bind with it three hairs from the cat's coat in a white

handkerchief, and bury all beneath a tree, hazel, oak, thorn or ash. Then you may feel confident that your new-found friend will stay with you.

If, whilst a ship is in harbour, a black cat comes aboard of its own free will, the same charm may be performed, the only difference being that the handkerchief may be thrown overboard, and the cat's three hairs combined with tobacco instead of the customary valerian.

The Cat Spell Oracle

If you would divine the future, it is lucky to call upon your cat as oracle. Frame the question clearly in your mind, then write it down three times. Whisper puss's magical name to yourself three times three, and speak the question three times aloud.

Now, making sure that the door is ajar, call to your cat. Carefully observe which forepaws appears first through the door as she walks into the room. If it is the left paw, a denial is your answer. If it is the right paw, 'yes' is your answer.

Having divined in this way, ponder the oracle's response. The key to its message, and what will transpire for the best, is within your own heart.

The Blackberry Cat Charm

If it should happen that your kitten was born of a
queen on Michaelmas Day, or just after its passing,
that little child-cat will be very lucky, and very
mischievous, up to naughty tricks all the livelong
day. If you own a blackberry cat, you will be both
blessed and tried in life, usually more so than
others. An old fable says the Devil fell down to
earth at Michaelmas, the feast day of St Michael
who is named after the Archangel of the Sun. The
Devil was said to have spoiled the blackberries by
his fall, though others say he made good wine. God
blesses the Devil, for he works under the auspices
of the Divine Being, and for the good of
humankind, although he achieves his good by
straining against us and going backwards.

Charm on Seeing a Cat

If a black cat should cross your path, you must greet the animal with courtesy, and stroke it if you can, whilst saying this charm:

'Black cat, cross my path,
Good fortune bring to home and hearth;
When I am away from home
Bring me luck where'er I roam.'

Bless the cat with the sign of the cross, and pass on your way. If you should abuse the cat, or ignore it, no good luck charm will be worked on your behalf.

Cat Dream Spell

If it should be that you dream of a cat, take note of these visions of your soul, for they have much to indicate to you.

If you dream of a black cat, that is lucky;
If you dream of a tortoiseshell cat, that is lucky in love;
If you dream of a ginger cat, that is luck in money and business matters;
If you should dream of a white cat, that means luck in prophecy, in learning lessons of the spirit, in

writing, inspiration, the creative arts, and all
spellworking, wisecraft, and woman's mysteries;
If you dream of a black-and-white cat, that means
luck with children, and in the conception of them;
If you dream of a tabby cat, that means luck for
your hearth and home, and for all therein;
If you dream of a grey cat, that means luck in
dreams, which will guide you and reveal treasured
secrets to you;
If you should dream of a multi-coloured cat, you
shall enjoy luck with friends, new and old.

Whenever you dream of a cat, it is sure to be a
lucky sign, unless the cat be a demon-cat, in which
case it is offering you a warning. Our folklore tells
us that cats are lucky creatures, whatever their
shade or colour.

May Kittens

If kittens are born in May, they come into the world at the time of the divine marriage of the God and the Goddess, and their souls are opened to many powers and much mystic knowledge. They need protection, and special blessing. Say this charm over them three times, and leave a laurel leaf where they sleep:

'May kittens, born as fays
Thrice I bless you as you lay;
May your souls aspire to heaven
May angels bless you seven times seven
May spirit of Nature walk with thee
So visions true and pure you see;
I crown you with this laurel leaf;
May you never come to grief.'

Then may you be sure that the teeth and the demon eyes of Darkness will never grasp them.

The Bride's Cat Spell

If a cat who is the queen or tom of the house, sneezes near the bride upon her wedding morning, that is a blessing, and she will know conjugal bliss. If the cat sneezes more than once, it foretells the number of children she will give birth to.

Angelic Charm for Protection and Good Fortune

If you would seek the help and protection of the angels, go by night to a wood or copse, over whose trees you can clearly see the rising moon. Bow to her three times, and then walk sunwise (clockwise) to make a magic circle. Stand in the centre of the ring, and kneel in reverence to the stars saying:

'Holy spirits Seraph, Kerun
Your brightness shines as one great sun
Angel Tharsis and highest Ariel
May your radiance in my heart dwell.'

Then turn towards home and, once there, summon puss and take her to your bedchamber. Repeat the ritual once more whilst she looks on, prepare for bed and retire at once, calling upon the cat by her magical name to strengthen your link with the angels, and to bless the working of your spell.

You may see your cat, and the four angelic spirits you have summoned, in your dreams that night. If so, you are doubly blessed.

Weather Spells

'Cat's-paw upon the water –
First sigh of Storm-King's daughter . . .'

(*from* Furies and Storm Spirits *by Sarah Greaves*)

Our human emotional inscape has, through the eyes of poets and artists, ever been objectified by the subtle humours of the weather and its theatrical phenomena. This is by no means only a poetical and literary viewpoint, however; folklore is rich in references to personified weather. Apart from the commonly known Jack Frost, Old Man Winter and the 'wind-dogs' of a rainbow broken by cloud, weather spirits abound, and each locality boasts its own, from the Cailleach Bheur of the Highlands who ushers in the cold weather and the snow, to the Dooinney-Oie, the Manx 'Night-Man' or 'Storm-Man' whose keening voice gives warning of coming storms.

Esoteric lore bears out this mystical understanding of the changing weather. It tells us that just as our bodies are composed of the four physical elements, so our minds and souls are composed from the subtle and refined spirits which give them life. Therefore, we can be overtaken by fire elementals (which make us angry and irritable), water elementals (which make us moody), air elementals (which cause detached dreaminess), and the elementals of earth (which can cause heavy, depressed and earth-bound feelings). The spirits of the elements cause the varying weather conditions which we see in physical manifestation from our viewpoint here on earth. Being aware of the forces alive within themselves, it was said that the ancient Druids could control the weather-elementals, and thus the weather itself.

Here again, the cat is friend and helper. The feline is thought to be able to commune with 'lunar spirits' and the salamanders, undines, sylphs and gnomes which comprise the four elementals. Its help in predicting the weather, and sometimes even in charming the weather-spirits, is invaluable.

It is possible to become something of a weather-prophet by studying the antics of cats, and the 'weather spells' which follow have all been meticulously observed and described over many centuries.

The cat is endowed with wisdom and intelligence, but is spared the encumbrances of reason and intellect, which separate the main body of humanity from a holistic sense of order in the world of nature which surrounds it. Cats are able to retain and maintain a mysterious empathy with the cosmos which we have lost over the years. Perhaps to begin in a small way, by observing cats and the weather, might help us to reclaim our forgotten heritage.

Charm to Make the Rain

In the time of Diana's moon, which is when it waxes towards full, you must find nine dry stones and sprinkle upon them droplets of water from a crystal bowl; and you must find a black, or a white, or yet a black-and-white cat to come and sit in the midst of them, even if she will stay only a few short moments, for her soul can make game with the lunar spirits, and coax the favour of rain from them.

After the cat has left the ring of stones, you must chant this rune in a whisper:

'Our Lady Mary
Queen of all the sea
Bring down the power
In this magical hour;
The sap rises in the tree
By the power of our Lady;
So shall the rain fall
At Our Lady's call
All thanks be
To Our Lady.'

By the grace of the Queen of all things, the drops will start to patter within an hour or two.

Storm-Omen

When your cat is restless to the point of something uncanny, frisking about the house hither and thither as though Old Nick himself were after her, be assured that stormy bustling winds are on their way; when she sits all calm and quiet and blinking the peace of her wisdom into the fire, then you know the storm is about to blow itself out.

How to Foretell a Fiery Night

When puss sleeps all day, it is because she is preparing for the night, which will be mysterious and lovely, lit up with fireballs and shooting stars. The stars will twinkle with vivacity, as though laughing and dancing in the skies, and there will be the breath of spirits and magic in the night-time garden, and in the wilds. On such a night, it is likely that puss will be out with the fairies until after dawn. Prophetic visions may be had from watching through the hours of such a night and communing with the spirits of the stars.

Rain Prophet

*'When puss washes behind her ears
We'll soon be tasting heaven's tears.'*

To Tell a Rain Spirit Is Near

When your cat rolls upon her back, and claws
playfully at the grass, twitching her tail and turning
up her eyes in skittish humour, you may discern
from her behaviour that a rain spirit is dancing
thereabouts, and will soon appear in corporeal form
as a swiftly-falling, drenching shower.

Spell to Tell the Advent of the Furies

When the cat of the household behaves like a
mischievous sprite, and will not settle nor be ruled,
and will not lie still even before the fire, she is
dancing with the air elementals, which are called
sylphs and which are the spirits of the wind. Soon,
as sure as eggs are eggs, a howling blast will start
up and make the fire roar in the chimney. The
storm-winds will last until the storm-man has
passed over and left his wild kiss upon the land;
only then will puss be calm and serene again, ready
to purr in tranquility before the fire.

The Face of The Moon Cat Spell

When your cat quietly contemplates the face of the moon, holding her pose as if she were a painting in soft, shadowed oils, and with eyes as big and shining as friar's lanterns, that means we shall have fair weather the next day, which will smile over the world from sunrise to sunset.

Rainbow Wishes Cat Spells

If you should see a rainbow, bending heaven's colours towards the dun earth, it is very lucky to call the cat of the house to you, and to stroke her three times from head to tail. Then you may make

three wishes upon the rainbow, which will be granted before the death of the old moon. You will also dream dreams of holiness and mystery, and your cat under the auspices of her magical name will guide you though their shining gates. If, as you watch, the rainbow billows and seems to break up as clouds are borne over it, these are wind-dogs, and on seeing them your cat will become restless.

To avert an ill omen, say to the wind-dogs:

'Dogs of the storm, this task perform,
Your falling rain must wash away harm.'

In this way, the wind-dogs are charmed against bringing bad luck.

Song by Starlight Cat Spell

If your cat should walk abroad under the stars, and seek high places, and give forth her caterwaul as if she could not help but strike up a cat's chorus, it is said that there will be boisterous weather with squalls of rain and distant thunder for three days.

Jack Frost Cat Spell

When puss sits with her back to the fire as though
she were a little statuette, except for the very tip of
her tail which twitches as though she were
watching for a mouse, that foretells a hard frost,
which will fall after midnight, and breathe a hoar of
white crystals where'er it creeps.

Two Fairy Spells

'When will you see fairies, my dear?
Before the cat can lick her ear . . .'

(nursery rhyme)

I n the twinkling of an eye, between one blink and
the next, it is said that fairies can sometimes be
seen. According to wiselore, fairies certainly
exist as dwellers in an ethereal dimension. To nurture a friendship with the fairies is rewarding but
painstaking work, as they are wary and suspicious
of humans. Yet they have many spiritual lessons to
impart, and our folklore gives myriad instances of
their favours and punishments. They will sometimes open a magical door into the human world
and allow us to see them for a moment, in order to
give lost travellers the right direction. People who
have experienced such guidance from the fairies
speak of such beings, not as vanishing, but of simply not being there any more after they have spo-
ken. Fairies admonish human avarice (which is
responsible for the pillage and destruction of the
kingdom of nature which they inhabit) in various
ways: by filling the pockets of the greedy with gold
which blows away as dead leaves when they try to
spend it, or concealing a precious stone or jewel

within an ugly or apparently useless article, confident that a person of good heart will find it. Wiselore teaches that such activities are not really to be considered as 'rewards' or 'punishment', but as a means of indicating spiritual truth.

Cats have ever been associated with the fairies, and it was often thought that if a brownie or other household spirit were present in the house, the cat would know and would communicate the intelligence to its owner. Communion with the spirit of a cat (as in, for example, the close companionship enjoyed between a favourite cat and its human friend) is said to facilitate human contact with the fairies and their ethereal world. One traditional method of achieving this was to call the cat into your dreams and allow its spirit to guide you to the fairy revels. Cats possess the qualities of stillness, silence, and patience, all three of which are vital in the pursuit of fairies!

The most favourable times for seeing fairies are the early hours of the morning, the noon hour, as evening falls, and midnight; the most favourable conditions are sunshine or the bright white light of a full moon (although any moonlit night is believed to vouchsafe visions of the fairy host). The 'fairy days' are traditionally Hallowe'en (31 October), Walpurgis Night (May Eve, 30 April), May Day, Midsummer Day (24 June) and its eve, Lady Day (25 March) and Christmas Day.

The Northern Lights Fairy Spell

When the firmament is alight with meteoric phenomena, and the Merry Dancers assume their pretty gowns and make great sport up and down the curtain of the night sky until they are in a fair frolic and frenzy, these Northern Lights are come to let you know that the evening is full of magic, and the season ripe for spells and craftworking.

Therefore, coax a cat (better if she be black) on to your lap, and sit alone with her in the garden, stroking her until a sheen appears on her coat, and she purrs contentedly. Have at your elbow a nipperkin of wine in a small vessel, and at the cat's first stretch, anoint her lightly with the wine, making the holy sign of the cross upon her head, and then do the same for yourself.

Gently grasp the end of her tail and stroke it three times swiftly over your left eye, and then over your right, saying:

'Elves of the night, enchant my sight,
Your forms for to see in moon or sunlight;
With this spell and with this sign
I pri'thee, forward my design.'

Let puss run off, and steal away to your
bedchamber, there to contemplate the moon and
the stars and all the magical lights of the sky from
your lattice. If you have found favour with the
fairies, then mystic dreams will come to you that
night, and afterwards you will begin to see the
Little People at their revels, faintly at first, but yet
more clear, more lucid, as the fairy-enchantment
blesses ever deeper your inner seeing.

The Fairy Cordial

To receive the grace of the fairies and to enter the
underworld and their mystic halls, you must watch
out for a bright moonlit night when puss seems
frisky and ardent, as if she were dancing with
spirits. If this is a night when the moon is full,
being Freya's moon, that is all the better. Just at the
rising of the stars, which is the time of Isis, you
must drink of a cordial which you will have ready
and waiting in your bedchamber. These shall be its
magical ingredients:
of mugwort – one chopped teaspoonful, of rue –

the same, of chicory – the same, of lavender – one teaspoonful, of valerian – one teaspoonful of the grated root.

Pour upon these a good cupful of boiling water, and bless the water as you pour it; and add a dash of honey, and three clover leaves, dried or fresh as may be.

Now leave the Fairy Cordial to stand before your window in the full flood of Freya's silvery moonlight, and if it should be that there is a mirror in which the draught is reflected, so much the better.

Now you must catch puss (with all respect and kindness) and bring her to your chamber, being yourself all ready for bed. Sit with her in the moonlight and slowly sip what remains of the Fairy Cordial, and tell her that you wish her to guide you in your dreams to the strange and lovely fairy worlds. Before you take your last sip of the potion, you must lift the cat up in your arms and bow to the moon, saying clearly:

'Freya, Lady of the Moon,
Grant to me, I pray, this boon:
This night do I appoint a guide
And to the fairy haunts would ride.

Guard me, for my heart is true;
Bless for me this magic brew;
May I never this night rue.'

Then drink the last few drops of the cordial, and
when you have done, tenderly remove the three
clover leaves and take them with you to bed.
Scatter a little rose-oil around your bed to make an
enchanted ring, and set puss at the end of your bed.
Now lie down, and when you are snug between the
sheets, place a clover leaf upon each eyelid and one
in the middle of your forehead. Say aloud:

'Aine, goddess of fairies,
Call my soul to Fairyland
Where'er that is.'

Last of all, you must whisper to puss that you wish
her to be your true guide, and you must fall into
sleep (which will come swiftly and sweetly), whilst
intoning her magical name into the soft robes of
your slumber as they enfold you.

And so it will be that you shall see the fairy halls
and the fairy kingdoms, if the magic be good; and
you shall dwell there in those hollow hills of
mystery it shall seem for years, though it shall be
but one night in the passing; and your heart shall
be pierced by their beauty and the power of their
knowledge; and when you return with your cat
companion, you and she share many secrets and
hidden visions of those regions, and your
communion will be deep and precious. But be
careful to tell the secret of the Fairy Cordial only to
those who bear true-hearted love and respect for
the fairies and for Elfame, for otherwise the journey
will be dangerous for them, and their own mocking
spirit will come home to plague and prate and
destroy their peace for many long years to come.

Heed this warning, and bide by its cautions, in all
your dealings with the Fairy Cordial.

List of Spells